THE FIGHT FOR DEMOCRACY

WITH AN ESSAY FROM
The Soul of Democracy,
The Philosophy of the World War
in Relation to Human Liberty
BY EDWARD HOWARD GRIGGS

By

J. A. HOBSON

First published in 1917

British Library Cataloguing-in-Publication Data
A catalogue record for this book is available
from the British Library

Man for the State means autocracy and imperialism;
MAN FOR MANKIND is the soul of democracy.

DEMOCRACY
AND SACRIFICE

AN ESSAY FROM
The Soul Of Democracy,
The Philosophy Of The World War
In Relation To Human Liberty
BY EDWARD HOWARD GRIGGS

We have seen the conflict of ideas in the War: the German philosophy that man exists for the state, the contrasting idea of democracy that the state exists for man. We may well ask why any institution should be regarded as sacred, except as it has the adventitious sacredness, coming from time, convention and hoary tradition. It was said long ago that "the Sabbath was made for man and not man for the Sabbath," and the statement may be universalized. Every institution on earth—marriage, the family, education, the church, the state—was made for man and not man for the institution. Humanity must always be the end. Why should we perpetuate any institution that does not serve life? Kant voiced the principle in his second imperative of duty: "Always treat humanity, whether in thine own person or that of any other, as an end withal, and never as a means only." Kant was a Prussian philosopher: one wonders what he would have thought of the "Kanonen-Futter" theory of manhood!

An organization or institution is only a machine, an instrument for a purpose. Thus always it is a means, never an end: its value lies in serving its purpose—the end of human life. So the whole existing order must justify itself. Where it rests on forms of injustice, it must be broken or destroyed, and there is no reason to fear the breaking.

Thus there is no "divine right" of kings. They represent a vested interest, surviving from the past. They must justify themselves by the service of those under them, or pass.

Similarly, there is no divine right of a class or caste, enjoying supremacy or special privilege. It also is a surviving vested interest, that must justify itself, or be swept aside as an incubus.

The same test applies to an empire. It, too, is a vested interest, developed out of conditions prevailing in the past. If it does not justify itself by the largest service of all within it, then it, too, is an anachronistic survival, no longer to be tolerated.

The principle is universal: the institution of private property, the controlling power of captains of industry, the capitalistic system, finally, the state itself, in every form: all are vested interests that may be permitted to continue in the exercise of power only as they prove their superiority to any other form of organization in serving the good of all.

This does not mean that, under democracy, the individual shall fail of sacrifice and the dedication to something higher than himself. That is the glory of life, transfiguring human nature, and without it, life sinks to sordid selfishness. Your life is worth, not what you have, but what you are, and what you are is determined by that to which you dedicate yourself. Is it creature comforts, pleasure, selfish privilege, or the largest life and the fullest service of humanity? What you have is merely the condition, the important question is, what do you do with it? Is it wealth, prosperity: do you sit down comfortably on the fact of it, to secure all the selfish pleasures possible; or do you regard your fortunate circumstances as so much more opportunity and obligation of leadership and service? Is it poverty, even starvation: do you whine and grovel, or stand erect, with shut teeth, andwring heroic manhood from the breast of suffering?

That is why peace can never be an end: it, too, is merely a condition or means. The question is, what do you do with your peace, for peace may mean merely sloth and cowardly ease, where war may mean unselfish heroism. That is what the peace promoters forget. War has its brutalities, and terrible indeed they are: unleashed hate, lust, cruelty and revenge; but war has its heroisms. It calls out the devotion to something higher than the individual from even the commonest of men. To-day all over the earth, ordinary men are quietly going out to probable death or mutilation in its most horrible forms, and going for the sake of an ideal larger than themselves. Women are doing even more than that. For it is not so hard to die, but to send out those you love, dearer than life itself, to almost certain death—that, indeed, is difficult, and women are doing it everywhere with a smile on their lips and choked-back tears.

Peace, on the other hand, has its virtues: the softening and refining of life, gradual development of sympathy, achievement of comfort and beauty; but peace has its vices. In times of peace and prosperity there seems to be no great cause at stake. Of course, always it is there, but we do not see it. We become increasingly absorbed in selfish interests, in the good of our immediate family. Thus petty, time-serving selfishness is the vice peculiarly characteristic of times of peace and prosperity. Consider, for instance, the spirit of France during the closing years of the nineteenth century, and at the present dark, but pregnant, hour of destiny.

Thus the question is not whether you have peace or war, but what you do with your peace or war. It is not whether you are rich or poor, but what you do with your riches or poverty.

Suppose we were able to reconstruct our entire social and industrial world, so that every human being would have plenty to eat, plenty to wear and a comfortable house to live in: would we have the kingdom of heaven? Not necessarily: we might have merely a comfortable, well-decorated pig-sty, if men lived to nothing higher than pigs. "Man cannot live by bread alone," important as bread is, but by dedication to the things of the spirit.

Thus there must ever be the capacity for self-forgetfulness, self-sacrifice, the dedication of life to supreme aims, but that does not mean the dedication of man to the institution. Rather it is the consecration to the welfare of humanity. Man for the State means autocracy and imperialism; Man for Mankind is the soul of democracy. That is the ideal to which we must rise, if democracy is to prove itself worthy to be the form of human society for the great future.

This ideal is realized through many lesser forms and instruments, but always with the same final test. The family, for instance, is one of these lesser forms, and the subordination of the individual to the family unit is just. Thus there is a measure of right in seeking first the interest of the family group; but when this is sought to the end of special privilege and debauching luxury, against the welfare of all, it becomes, as we have seen, an evil.

There is, similarly, a certain justice in the subordination of the individual to the social class or group interest. It is right that artisans should unite in trade unions, that employers should get together in associations for common benefit. One need only contrast the conditions where each workman had to bid in competition against all others, and each manufacturer, the same, to realize the advance made through group union and cooperation. When either group, however, seeks to further its own interest at the expense of the welfare of the whole society, as in securing class legislation, achieving monopolies, holding efficient workers to the level of production of the slowest and least capable of the group, then the class or group spirit becomes an evil that must be fought for the good of all.

It is exactly the same with the nation. Its interest is justly served only in harmony with the welfare of humanity. Any current problem will illustrate the principle, as, for instance, that of immigration.

Certainly the nation has the right to prohibit immigration which produces unassimilated plague-spots and threatens to cause racial deterioration, as in phases of Oriental immigration to the Pacific coast. Similarly, it is right to restrict immigration that would further economic prosperity, at the expense of the manhood of the nation. We must answer the question, whether we want factories or men. It is desirable to have some of both, of course, but when one is to be obtained at the expense of the other, it is manhood that must be the deciding end.

On the other hand, when it comes to refusing a refuge to the poor and oppressed, who are physically and morally acceptable, but lack a small amount of money, or are unable to respond to a literary test, then the welfare of humanity demands the opposite decision. Better give them the fifty dollars—a healthy slave was worth more than that in the old days. So teach them to read and write. The nation, can readily pay the small economic price and accept the incidental difficulties for the sake of the larger end.

Thus the deciding principle must always be the welfare, happiness, growth, intelligence, helpfulness of each individual in harmony with all others. Humanity is incarnatein each man. While, therefore, the individual must dedicate and, at times, sacrifice himself, it is for the sake, not of the state, church or other institution, but for the welfare of all—*Man for Mankind.*

From so many sources the view finds expression that modern life has been "weakened by humanitarianism." If there is truth in the view, we would better take account of it and radically revise our ethical philosophy. If it is false, it is a damning error, the reiteration of which tends to undermine all that has been achieved for the spirit.

An interesting comment on the view is the fact that, in spite of all its horrors, this War has given *no attested instance of arrant cowardice on any front.* Cruelty, lust, brutality, hate: these have appeared in unspeakable guise, but apparently no cowardice or weak timidity; yet the mail clad heroes of ancient wars, who met their adversaries face to face, were subjected to no such strain as the men standing in trenches waiting momentarily death or mutilation from an unseen foe. No, modern life has not lost strong fiber and is capable of supreme heroism.

The old society secured its leadership through *noblesse oblige*—the obligation of nobility. Men of aristocratic family and rank felt that, because they stood above the people, they owed a certain leadership and service, and they gave it, often in abundant measure, but always condescendingly from above.

We have lost "noblesse oblige": we may even be glad it is gone, if we can substitute for it something larger and better. It is not the obligation of nobility, but the obligation of humanity that is the need: to realize that all power is obligation. As you can, you owe; and as you know, you owe. If you have money, it is so much obligation of leadership and service. If you have talent, education, social or political influence, it is all so much obligation of leadership and service. If, as individuals, we can generally realize that and act upon it, then indeed we may hope to carry to successful completion the experiment of democracy and see our beloved country fulfill the measure of moral leadership to which we believe she is called among the nations of the earth, but fulfilling it not as master over slave, nor as one empire among others, but as a more experienced brother toward others following the same open path.

PREFACE

The experiences of the war have thoroughly exposed
the delusion that democracy in any of its essential
features has been yet attained in Great Britain. Few
of the elements of civil and personal liberty have stood
secure, while political self-government by popular
representation has been put on to the scrap-heap. The
industrial liberties won for the organised workers by
generations of sacrifice and struggle have been similarly
cancelled. The patriotic sentiment of the people has
been deliberately exploited by the enemies of
democracy. Their fears and suspicions have been
allayed by the pretence that the invasions of their
liberties were only "for the duration of the war," and
that they would get them back with interest after-
wards. But those who realise that this war has been
the opportunity which every cause of oligarchy and
reaction has been waiting for, in order to fasten the
fetters of political and economic serfdom more firmly
on to the limbs of "the masses," will take a different
view of the prospects of democracy after the war.
They will recognise that democracy has abandoned
many positions it had won, that its enemies are more
strongly entrenched than before, and that they can
only be dislodged by a general and well organised

attack on all the fortresses of power, privilege and property in politics, industry and society. Democracy is not "inevitable." It will not come of its own accord. It will have to be fought for and won. And in order that the fight may be conducted with success it is necessary to know the forces and the tactics of the enemy. With this object in view I have endeavoured to provide a survey of the battlefield, showing the various forces of capitalism, conservatism, militarism, imperialism, protectionism, bureaucracy, with their intellectual and spiritual allies and mercenaries, and to indicate the most advantageous methods of attacking these enemies of the people. The fuller survey of the situation is contained in a volume which will appear this autumn under the title of "Democracy After the War" (to be published by Messrs. Allen and Unwin). This booklet contains the last section of that book. If its exposition is not always simple, I would plead in extenuation that the issues involved are themselves complex, and that the enemies of democracy rely upon this very complexity to confuse the mind and distract the counsels of the people.

J. A. HOBSON.

Hampstead,
   June, 1917.

CONTENTS

CHAPTER I.

How to Break the Vicious Circle.

In face of the array of reactionary forces, what tactics are the defenders of liberty, democracy, and social progress to pursue? So formidable is the enemy, so strong his actual hold upon the instruments of power, as to render it unthinkable that he will yield to any merely instinctive revolt against the new shackles imposed upon our liberties, or to any blind movement of economic discontent. There must be a considered policy of attack. In that consideration the first need is to understand the nature of the bond of alliance between the reactionary forces. Nor is it enough to realise the general character of the interests and secret sympathies which have drawn them together. We must understand that we are dealing with a vicious circle. This term is commonly applied in logic to a bad process of reasoning, the badness of which consists in arguing that A leads to B and B to C, the accepted conclusion—without perceiving that it may with equal reason be held that C leads to A. In discussions upon the principles of social reform the common illustration is found in the contention between the Individualist and the Socialist as to the validity of proposed reforms. The Individualist contends that poverty is mainly due to defects of personal character, and argues that reforms in social environment are unattainable without preceding improvements in personal intelligence and morale, and that even were reforms imposed from outside they

would be inefficacious.   To this the Socialist replies by
pointing out that personal intelligence and morale
cannot be improved while the environment remains
what it is.   " You must first," he urges, " improve the
environment, then you will get your improvement in
character," while the Individualist once more retorts
that the very desire and so the power to effect improvements of environment imply a prior improvement of
character.   So the argument goes waltzing round.

The circle of reaction which confronts Democracy
will be quite as vicious and more complex in its
arrangement.   The point at which we enter is
the militarist bureaucracy that will be in control of
affairs when the war is brought to an end, with
conscription in being and great emergency powers
exercised by the Government over industry and the
civil life of the people.   How are the people to get
back the civil liberties they have lost and to restore
and strengthen their powers of self-government?   The
retention of conscription and of exceptional legislative
and executive powers in the hands of a self-appointed
oligarchy will be defended on the ground that peace
is precarious and the international situation so grave
that an immediate return to free institutions and
constitutional forms of government is dangerous to
national defence.   If the reactionists have their way
peace will have been made precarious, and the international situation kept grave, by a settlement based
on military, naval, and economic force and containing
elements of insecurity.   The dangers of industrial and
civil disorder, arising from the economic processes of
resettlement, and graver on account of the precarious
international situation, will be adduced as a second
reason for the retention of emergency powers for the
government.

If this menace is to be averted, the peoples must be
able to insist upon an international settlement not
containing the seeds of future wars, and a League of

Nations, operated not on lines of class diplomacy, but in accordance with the mutual interests of the constituent peoples. So, likewise, in dealing with the difficulties of economic reconstruction, a genuinely representative policy must displace the action of a definitely capitalist State operated by official dictators and a few captured and servile " labour leaders." In other words, political and economic democracy must be able to assert itself with vigour and success. But how can it be possible that, amid the confusion of returning peace, the political and economic organisations of the people, impaired or lapsed for the duration of the war, can become so much more powerful as to insist not merely on the resumption of all pre-war liberties, but on the displacement of class supremacy in foreign policy by the principles and *personnel* of popular government? For nothing less than this democratic control of foreign policy will suffice. Leave this single sphere of oligarchy, it is now made manifest that all other forms of popular self-government are worthless. For the class that controls foreign policy controls the supreme issue of peace or war, and through that controls expenditure on armaments, issues of conscription, and the direction given to industrial and commercial developments, education, and the intellectual, moral, and recreational life of the people. If, therefore, democracy is to be anything more than an idle name, given to a finally impotent vote cast once in each five years, the test struggle will be fought around the fortress of foreign policy. For, retaining that fortress, the capitalist oligarchy will always be able to win back any losses it may have sustained in the control of domestic politics during peace time, by rousing the fear or, in the last resort, the actual peril of another war.

But how can the people in this or other capitalist countries make themselves strong enough to win the real control of their external and internal policy? We

say that if they could be brought to a realising sense
of the danger of their situation, and the urgent necessity of organising so effectively as to give real meaning
to the formal power which numbers possess, success
would be theirs.   But here we collide against another
power of the reaction.   The people, as a whole, have
not the intelligence, the knowledge, and the persistent
will needed to make democracy effective for this great
task.   Why not?   Not because of any congenital
incapacity to think, to learn, and to exert will power
in seeking their ends, but because the circumstances
under which they live and work, and the arts of
management of public opinion by the ruling and
possessing classes, preclude them from acquiring and
exercising the intellectual and moral powers which are
needed.   The poverty of the poor and the wealth of the
rich conspire to make democracy impossible.   Disabled
by a life of toil amid depressing surroundings for the
effort of clear thought and effective co-operation for
large, complex, and distant action, the mass of workers
are distracted and beguiled by the " organs of public
opinion," which play upon their credulity and their
lighter tastes and interests so as to keep them from
any form of organisation that is really dangerous to
the powers above.   In other words, the operation of
economic forces under capitalism prevents the public
from realising adequately the dangers and injustices
from which they suffer, and from exerting the will
power requisite for organising so as to apply effective
remedies.   So we are brought to the orthodox Socialist
position.   Capitalism is the enemy—capitalism, with
its monopoly of wealth, leisure, and intelligence, and
its power to use these privileges not only to rob the
labourer of a large portion of the product of his labour,
but so to enfeeble and enslave his mind as to prevent
him from organising any effective rebellion.   But how
can these powers of capitalism be broken, except by
means of that very organisation of political and

economic democracy which they are employed to crush? So the vicious circle is once more closed. Military oligarchy is linked to secret class diplomacy, the fruits of this foreign policy involve conscription and vast expenditure on armaments, thus precluding effective advances in those services of educational and social reform which would render possible a democratic organisation competent to overthrow the forces of capitalism which sustain, direct, and feed upon the strong military State. The mechanical analogy of an endless chain is not adequate. For the vicious circle is organic and alive. It is a poisonous co-operative interplay of parasitic organisms, feeding on the life of the peoples by mastering and perverting to their own base purposes the political, economic, and moral activities of humanity. Political oligarchy, industrial and financial capitalism, militarism, intellectual and spiritual authoritarianism, find natural allies in the servile press, the servile school, the servile church, which they utilise to drape their selfish dominion with the gallant devices of national service, imperialism, " scientific management," and other cloaks for class-mastery.

The following diagram will roughly serve to illustrate the nature of the circle of reaction, though it goes a very little way towards representing the intricacy of the mutual interplay of material and spiritual interests by which the reactionary factors are related to one another.

It is, however, so important to realise the nature of the bonds of sympathy and mutual support among members of the circle that we may profitably recite the part played by such a typical force of reaction as Protectionism.

By Protectionism is meant the utilisation of politics by trades for special economic gain through restriction of free markets. Of Protectionism, the tariff is the leading instrument. Now Protectionism enjoys a direct community of interest or sympathy with almost

THE VICIOUS CIRCLE OF REACTION.

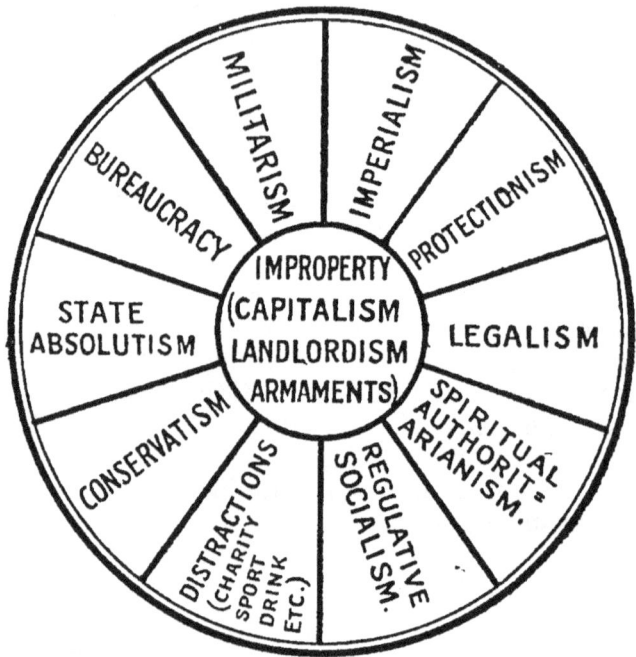

every other member of the circle, even those which seem at first sight most remote from its commercial aims. Its connection with the economic taproot, Improperty or Capitalism, is of course the closest: for its essential activity consists in looting the unprotected consumer and the weaker trades for the benefit of the strongly organised capitalist trades. It connects with Imperialism, partly by retaining and incorporating remnants of the old policy of Mercantilism, partly by attaching itself by special modification of structure to the sentimental and political design of a united self-sufficing Empire. It appeals to Bureaucracy, State Absolutism, and the wider spirit of Authoritarianism in various ways. Bureaucracy it conciliates by offering a large province for the control of expert officialism, the formation and administration of a " scientific

tariff,'' power, "honours," and lucrative appointments. State Absolutism (Prussianism) it nourishes
and conciliates by fostering a distinctly national
economy and by its hostility to economic and political
Internationalism. It connects with Militarism, partly
by the special requirements of the armament and
related trades in their capacity of key-industries needing
protection and other State aids as instruments of
national defence, partly by the emotional sympathy
obtained through representing trade in terms of
economic war. Trade, falsely imagined as a struggle
between rival States, serves to feed and inflame international animosities and to sow the seeds of militarism
and war. With the State policy, here designated
"regulative Socialism," Protectionism has a close
affinity. In modern Protectionist countries protection
is sought, not only through tariffs, but in various forms
of subsidy and other legal or administrative aids given
to home or export trade in railroad and shipping
facilities, etc. A still closer attachment has been
formed in Australia by fastening tariff regulations to
a labour policy of guaranteed wages and pensions, an
experiment very likely to be proposed in this country
as a means of buying the support of Labour for the
new Protectionist designs of Capitalism. The bonds
which attach Protection to Conservatism are so strong,
so numerous, and so evident as to require no close
analysis. It may here suffice to say that Protectionism, as a form of capitalistic exploitation, requires
Conservatism as the natural defender of the vested
interests it creates. Finally, Protectionism makes an
easy appeal to every other obscurantist, bellicose, and
reactionary element. The spirit of the public-house,
the racecourse, the music hall, and the "yellow press"
so easily accords with the presentation of trade as a
competitive struggle between nations as to close the
door to any recognition of its true co-operative
character.

In similar fashion we could trace the network of common interests and sympathies which connect any other member of the circle, such as imperialism, bureaucracy, academic education, landlordism, legalism, with all the other members, thus weaving the whole number into one effective organic confederation of reactionary powers, each rallying to the support of any other that is attacked, each continually engaged in adding material strength and moral prestige to the others.

I have laboured at some length the analysis of this unholy alliance in order that defenders of democracy may realise the number and the resources of their enemy. For, until these are realised, democracy can evolve no tactics adequate to safeguard any of the liberties it still retains, much less to make new advances in the establishment of the power of the peoples. For if my analysis is correct, none of the single and simple remedies devised by political or economic reformers will meet the needs of the case. Attack the fortress of secret diplomacy, say some. The democratic control of foreign policy is the key to salvation. But how can this be done when the vicious foreign policy is sustained by social and political forces rooted in Capitalism? Well, says the Socialist, you must first attack and overthrow Capitalism. Capitalism is the tap-root from which all the other branches of reaction derive their nutriment. Protectionism and Imperialism are special modes of profiteering in which the powers of the State are handled by business interests for business ends. The secret processes of foreign policy are mainly engaged in promoting commercial and financial objects, and militarism and navalism are instruments in their pushful profiteering. Moreover, Militarism and Navalism are themselves great and increasingly profitable branches of Capitalism. Regulative and Concessive Socialism is oil to lubricate the wheels of Capitalism. The Law, the Church, the

Press, the Universities, the Bureaucratic State itself, are in the last resort the mercenary defenders of the capitalist system. Even emollients and distractions, such as drink and the amusement trades, are great capitalistic enterprises out for monopoly gains. Cut out from business the profiteering motive and the forms of improperty which accrue, and all the other organs of reaction would wither and collapse.

It is a specious proposal, that of a single concentrated attack on Capitalism as a profiteering system. But it is not practicable. For it ignores two factors in the situation. The first is that many of the forces of reaction have strong supports in personal and social motives of interest, power and prestige, independent of their alliance with Capitalism. The second is that Socialism, national or international, is not really able to approach, much less to overthrow, Capitalism, because of the powerful defences—political, moral, and intellectual—by which it is encompassed. Socialism has neither a concerted feasible tactic nor a sufficient number of able, trusted leaders in close intellectual and political agreement, nor a large enough body of enthusiastic, convinced, and indivisible followers. The patriotic stampede of Socialism in every country in the summer of 1914 is as convincing a testimony to its inadequacy to the task of overthrowing Capitalism as could possibly be given. This inadequacy will not disappear until Socialism ceases to isolate and over-stress the economic class-war. I do not depreciate the importance of this aspect of the great democratic struggle. But if social democracy is to deserve its title and to realise its meaning, it must broaden its outlook and its policy. If Capitalism were a really separable phenomenon in the analysis of reactionary power, then Socialism might sustain its limited rôle of concentrating all its efforts, economic and political, upon its destruc-tion. But when Capitalism is understood as only one, albeit the most important, member of a confederacy

of reactionary forces, each with other evil sources of
power besides the nourishment it gets from Capitalism,
the task of overthrowing it must be expanded into the
broader task of establishing democracy.   The people
cannot successfully attack any stronghold of Capitalism
unless they control their State, both its legislative and
administrative services, for otherwise the assailed
interests will use the weapons of the State to ward off
their attack.   The people cannot even plan an effective
attack on Capitalism until they have the education and
the understanding to direct their attack, not at some
obvious and superficial abuse of employers' powers,
but at the vitals of their enemy.   How long a time,
for example, it takes for a working-class Socialist
movement to realise that the heart of modern Capitalism is the credit system and that the socialisation of
credit is the most important means of undermining
Capitalism !

If, therefore, the people are to deal effectively with
the circle of reaction, they must strike simultaneously,
not at one, but at many points.   They cannot say
Capitalism is the most formidable enemy, therefore
we will dispose of that first, and then we will take
possession of the State, and conquer, one by one, the
means of education, the press, and the other members
of the circle.   A vicious circle cannot be broken in this
way.   The full spirit of democracy must be roused,
organised, and directed to a general attack.   After this
war every cause of popular progress will be endangered,
every liberty menaced.   Hitherto the reforming spirit
and the progressive movement in society have drifted
into barren specialism.   This has been the temptation
of the " practical " reformer, the desire to achieve
some single, definite early result by confining his
reforming energy to some narrow manageable line of
activity.   The interrelation between all reforms has
even helped to bring about this wasteful economy.   For
it has enabled the specialist to represent his speciality

as the source or the essential condition of every other reform. The single-taxer, for example, has been able to find in his specific a full social gospel, economic, political, and moral, the sufficient basis of a new ideal human order. The free trader, even now, often exhibits his principle and policy as a panacea for all national and international troubles, and as an adequate security for liberty and justice. The educational enthusiast is easily persuaded that trained individual character and intelligence are the only or prior conditions of every genuine reform, and that social salvation can come about in no other way. But even he is undercut by the temperance or the housing specialist, who believes that the destruction of the drink habit or the better hygiene of the home is necessary to give education or any other higher desire or activity an opportunity of growth. Within the last two generations there has been a great uprising of reform energy in the churches, the political parties, the Labour movement, in organised science and philanthropy. But it has been for the most part sterilised by the same practical fallacy, *i.e.*, the belief that early tangible results could best be got by separatist action, by each group " doing its bit " in the work of social reform. Every one of these reforms is necessary. But every one of them is inimical to some one or more powerful vested interest, material or moral, and is suspected by the general body of conservatism and reaction. Thus its separate endeavour to redress a particular grievance or to promote a particular advance has been crushed or made innocuous by some trifling policy of concessions. Reaction, motived by some inner impulse of co-operation, presents a solid front against such particularist attacks. Finding its enemy divided, it triumphs. If democracy is to have a chance of winning it can only be by the union of all those genuinely progressive forces which have hitherto acted apart. But here comes the difficulty. They must perceive the necessity of common action. This means a widening of intellectual outlook and of sympathy. The single-taxer, the temperance reformer, the educationalist, the free trader, the trade unionist, the Socialist must become, in fact and feeling, before all else, a democrat. He must have a vision of the whole scope of what is involved in democracy and the struggle to achieve it, and be willing to put his specialism into the common movement. Possibly the term and concept democracy, by common usage, give an undue prominence to the distinctively political aspect of the movement, just as Socialism is apt to do to the economic aspect. But I choose democracy as the expression of the wider aims because it makes the appeal to the power of a self-directing people, operative in industry, in government, and in all the institutions and activities of social life, as the goal of co-operative endeavour and the instrument for the attainment or support of all the special forms through which the common life finds expression.

The whole object of this somewhat laborious analysis of reactionism has been to show the unity of the apparently unrelated reactionary forces, and thereby to reveal the necessity of co-ordination among the forces of democracy. If we can show the keen land reformer that he cannot in fact gain his object except by throwing his energies into the broad movement to recover and enlarge the liberties of the people; if we can make the educationalist, the temperance man, the "social purist," the hygienist, the franchise leagues, and the other specialists recognise that they also can only make progress to their desired goal by perceiving and feeling its organic unity with the general cause of democracy, we shall for the first time begin to realise that hitherto baffling hope which has deluded several generations of democrats, the power of numbers. Democracy has never yet had this power, its friends as well as its enemies have always succeeded in dividing the mass mind and the mass energy by canalising it into innumerable feeble, isolated, or conflicting channels.

If the experiences of this war have not revealed this fatal error, and the necessity of expelling from all specialist progressive movements those elements which are unable to take the wider outlook and to respond to the larger intellectual appeal, we can only conclude that our people is incapable and, therefore, unworthy of democracy. If they can still submit to be hood-winked and bamboozled by sham forms of political representation, by industrial controls which leave them no determinant voice in the most vital issues of work and livelihood, by organs of "public opinion" in which the public have no initiative, by social sedatives and distractions designed to keep them quiet and innocuous, there is nothing to be done except to dismiss from our minds the vision of democracy as an idle phantasm of a disordered imagination. But, before submitting to this dismal judgment, those who entertain the larger vision must at least make their appeal to the leaders of the specialist reforms. I do not despair of this appeal. Many of the active spirits in the movements of peace, temperance, housing, land, franchise, and other specialisms are attached to more than one reform, and have been feeling their way to co-operation with kindred bodies. Inside many of the churches the Catholic spirit has been gaining on the particularist in the movement towards a more liberal theology, a closer spiritual communion, and a common social ethic. Even in the older political parties in this and other countries, modern thought has been operating as a dissolvent of the accepted class creeds and barriers. Active-minded men and women have been sitting more loosely by their institutions and attachments. The critical spirit has been abroad. The rapid ferment of thought and feeling on the status of woman and sex problems during recent years has been at once an index and a source of revolutionary energy directed to the very foundations of society. Coincident with the new and startling ebullitions of revolt in the world of Labour, this new sex consciousness has transformed the whole nature of social discontent, and helped to turn it into broader channels. The shattering experiences of war will have broken the taboos and sanctities which warded off close scrutiny into the basic institutions of State, Property and Industry, the Family, Religion, and Morals. A new tide of scepticism and audacious experiment will surge against all the pillars of the' accepted social order, meeting in turbulent opposition to the drift of war-weary and conservative forces towards the shelter of the old grooves. Millions of minds to which these basic institutions were unreal abstractions, with no actual bearing for good or evil on their lives, will have learnt differently. Hard personal experience will have taught them what an instrument of destruction and oppression a State may be. The sanctity of property, industrial liberty, family life, standards of consumption, will have been subjected to violent and even paralysing shocks. That an act of politics can bring death and desolation into a million homes, that all the common habits and liberties of men and women can suddenly be cancelled by official orders, that all the natural and accepted precepts of religion and morality can be violated or reversed at the call of national emergency will have been a revelation of huge, unsuspected perils, in the midst of which the peoples have been slumbering. All live minded men and women must perceive how foolish and futile are the little political, social, religious, or philanthropic causes into which they have put their zeal so long as these controlling institutions of society remain so radically defective in structure and control. Our hope lies in the conviction that the fierce light of war and its glowing aftermath will show men that unless an ordered popular will can flood all the main channels of national life, intelligently controlling all the major organs of government and influence, State, economic system, Church, press, schools, and universities, and the recreative and relief adjuncts, there is and can be no security for anything that ordinary men and women value in life. The exposure of sham democracy in the " liberal nations " will have been complete. If the lesson is not learned, it will be because the ignorance or stupidity of the peoples is invincible. To divide and to distract have been the methods by which the forces of reaction have made democracy a sham. Unity and continuity of effort alone can make democracy a reality.

CHAPTER II.

THE NEW ECONOMIC SITUATION.

One of the most subtle defences of conservatism has been the modern notion, sedulously sown, that democracy was a process so inevitable and predestined in the evolution of society that no clearly conscious and purposive direction was required. Marxism embodied this false belief in its "scientific" view of the evolution of industry, and its political counterpart has flourished most vigorously in the optimism of the ordinary "good" American. The dissipation of this delusion should be one of the chief services of this war. Democracy cannot be brought about by a drift or tendency of unconscious purpose, it needs conscious organisation and direction by the co-operative will of individuals and nations. Until this co-operative will has been created and made effective, it must continue to remain an open question whether democracy is possible. The method of this conscious operation of the human will is therefore the issue of first practical importance. Now, though I have striven to point out the necessity of organising the democratic will so as to attack not one or two but many points in the vicious circle of reaction, this tactic is consistent with a certain amount of concentration upon one or two positions of outstanding strength. In this sense it is true that the main attack needs to be made upon the vested interests of improperty in the control of politics and industry after the war.

Several definite issues related to economic reconstruction must come up without delay into the forefront of the battle. The first demand will be that the State shall not suddenly or rapidly let down the volume of demand for labour by stopping public expenditure at a time when the labour markets will be flushed by a rapid return of men from the fighting forces into industry. During the latter part of the war more than half the wage-earners will have been directly or indirectly employed in providing goods and services for the State. Any rapid cessation of this demand for labour would not merely bring about a temporary turmoil, as the displaced workers were scrambling for private jobs, but would create a far graver situation, supposing that private employment did not expand as largely or as rapidly as was needed to absorb the displaced workers, together with the returning soldiers. Now it would be extremely foolish for the Government to rely upon any such expansion of private employment. For though the needs for great activity in all economic departments, agriculture, mining, shipbuilding, the staple manufactures, transport and commerce, so as to replace the destruction and wastage of the war and to furnish to the world those numerous supplies which have been withheld or constricted for several years, ought to stimulate to full activity all the available labour and capital resources of this and other nations, we cannot assume their smooth and effective operation. A dangerous or obscure international situation, involving great difficulties in forecasting the new trade currents, will disable manufactures and trades engaged in overseas trade from planning production and forecasting prices with any confidence, or in obtaining the credit necessary to carry on their enterprises. Even in internal trade, the disturbances in distribution of wealth and in methods of production and consumption produced by the war, will leave their impress in new risks and a more speculative situation. The whole financial system of the world will be left quivering with the shocks of war, and the changes in ownership of securities will have unforeseen effects upon the exchanges. While, therefore, we may predict that great efforts will be made to produce large quantities of ships, rails, and other forms of wealth destroyed by war, to repair the public and private plant which has been allowed to fall into disrepair, to resume with great activity the suspended building trades, and to restore the depleted stocks of foods, clothing, and other articles, this resumption of private enterprise cannot be relied upon to meet the urgency of the situation. Even if the required plant and material were available (which in many cases would not be the case), and labour were present in abundance, the vital factor of business confidence is likely to be lacking.

In fact it is self-evident that any sudden lapse from the State Socialism of war-time, with its enormous Governmental control of engineering, agriculture, mining, transport, and other vital industries, and its correspondingly enlarged expenditure, to the pre-war conditions, would spell disorder and disaster. The State must continue to retain a large proportion of this control and this spending power if unemployment, industrial depression, a fall of wages, and something like social revolution are to be averted. If the Government were suddenly to stop its war contracts or to reduce them with great celerity, there is no reason to believe that the enormous expenditure on labour which they represent would automatically be transferred to private enterprise.

An instinct of self-preservation will, therefore, impel the State to endeavour to retain after the war many of the emergency powers it has acquired during the war. Much of this retention will have the support of popular opinion. Though wealthy tax-payers and financial parasites may demand an early reduction of public expenditure to something like the pre-war level, the obvious necessity of safeguarding employment will support the alternative of maintaining a large volume of State expenditure directed from war services to peace services, *i.e.*, to the performances of those great constructive services of social security and progress which hitherto the State has been too impoverished or too cowardly to undertake. It will henceforth be impossible for any Government to say that the country cannot afford the money needed to house the people and to educate their children properly, to supply free medical and legal services, adequate provision for old age and unemployment, to develop the resources of the land, set up small holders, improve the roads and canals, and assist the municipalities in town-planning and public recreation.

It is true that the State Socialism of the war has been assisted by conditions of public feeling not available for ordinary times. People have been willing to pay taxes, tolerate official interferences, work more energetically and more smoothly, from patriotism and a sense of public danger. Much of the old distrust of the State, and particularly its fiscal exactions, will return with peace. Revelations of official blundering, extravagance, and corruption will be rife throughout the business world. Both among the employing and the working classes there will be a disposition to shake off the new fetters. But that disposition will be countered and overborne by the pressure of new economic and political movements. Though many of the irksome and unpopular powers of the State in the way of sumptuary laws and police regulations will doubtless disappear, the general development of State economic functions will remain. The war will have advanced State Socialism by half a century. The national control of railways and the unification of the railway system cannot be undone, and must lead to complete nationalisation. The coal and iron mines of the country and the coal trade are not likely to return to pre-war conditions. Together with such trades as engineering, shipbuilding, and chemicals, they will be recognised as national industries, in the sense that the Government will be made responsible for ensuring their best productivity, satisfactory conditions for labour, and reasonable prices. Whether the performance of these obligations entails public ownership and management, or is consistent with some system of cartels or syndicates, with State representation and suzerainty, remains an open question. But, in any case, the old condition of private profiteering, with a fluctuating policy of cut-throat competition and secret combination, cannot return. Nor is it less certain that State Socialism will make a distinct invasion into the domain of landed property and agriculture. The development of domestic food supplies, the encouragement of a rural population, schemes of afforestation and reclamation of waste lands, town planning, taxation of land values, as an instrument of local and national revenue, must all contribute to this end. War experience will probably not leave the liquor trade in private hands. The experience of finance during the last three years will have brought the issues of national banking and national insurance into the forefront of practical State Socialism. It will no longer be considered safe or expedient to allow the supply of money, in its modern form of credit, to be regulated by the arbitrary will of bankers and financiers for their personal gain, with the right to call upon the State to rescue them in times of peril and to place huge war profits to their private accounts. The nationalisation of banking and insurance should be a natural outcome of the new situation.

These two extensions of the functions of the State for
 (1) The supply of fuller public services to the people in their general capacity of producer-consumers ;
 (2) The enlargement of State ownership and administration in various special economic fields

—will necessarily be accompanied by a third extension in the shape of a large increase of taxing power. However successful the State may prove itself to be in the administration of the new public businesses and properties it takes over, it is not likely that they can advantageously be made to contribute more than a small share of the costs of the new State. One of the sharpest and most controversial issues which must arise after the war will, therefore, relate to methods of taxation. The need of providing the interest and sinking fund for the war borrowing, the heavy temporary costs of demobilisation and industrial re-settlement, the permanent pensions fund, and the maintenance, for some years, at any rate, of an expenditure on armaments higher than the pre-war level, will require a yield from taxes at least as high as the 550 millions estimated to be the yield for 1916-17. *Primâ facié*, the bulk of this taxation must be imposed upon the well-to-do, the "capitalist" classes. It will, however, be to their interest to shift as much of it as they can on to the workers by indirect taxation, accompanied by a reduction of the income tax exemption limit, so as to bring in the better paid artisans, miners, and other workers who, to meet the rise of prices, have secured higher money wages. The chief indirect taxation proposed by the capitalists will take the shape of protective duties upon imports. Protection will, of course, have this double advantage for the capitalists. It will relieve them of a portion of the taxes which otherwise must come out of their pockets and put it on the working class consumers. But it will confer on them the greater gain of better combination for control of the national market and the enlarged profits derived from the raised prices at which they will be able to sell their whole supplies. Thus the manufacturing, agricultural, and trading interests not mainly dependent upon export trade will make a vigorous attempt to put high Protection on the country under the guise of national security, imperial unity, punishment of Germany, and maintenance of the Alliance. If they can succeed in this design, and can keep down vexatious State interference with the new combinations which the war experiments backed by tariffs will enable them to form, they may be able to shift on to " the masses " a large proportion of the burden of taxation. If this project were launched under its own name and alone it would have no chance of success. In vain is the net spread within the sight of any bird. It will, therefore, be necessary to try to divide democracy and to protect Protection by surrounding it with other more attractive appeals to Labour. This will be done by the new Prussian-Australianism which Mr. Lloyd George will probably introduce, and for which he will secure the support of his captured Labour men. By Prussian-Australianism I mean a combination of the capitalist-bureaucratic organisation of industry and commerce practised in modern Germany with the Nationalist-Labour policy of Australia. What our capitalists will want is Protection and high productivity of labour. This high productivity they now know to be technically and humanly feasible, provided they can get the assent of the workers to continue after the war the suspension of regulations restricting output and to accept dilution and other improvements in the organisation of labour. In order to purchase these conditions of profitable Capitalism, the State, in direct co-operation with syndicates of employers, will probably propose a system of guaranteed standard wages, unemployed insurance, and pensions, with some joint boards of national industry for the settlement of issues affecting the welfare of Labour. Even the capitalists of the great export trades, who do not favour Protection, will support the main structure of this Prussian-Australianism as the best method of securing the harmonious and profitable working of Capitalism under the new order.

CHAPTER III.

Two Problems for Labour.

This new situation, arranged by a skilful coalition of capitalists and politicians, will present two problems of supreme importance to democracy. What attitude shall the workers adopt towards proposals for increased productivity? What attitude towards the State as controller of industry? These two problems, as will presently be shown, are not independent of one another. But it will be well to approach them by the way of the demand for higher productivity. Now here, at the outset, we are met by deep suspicion on the part of Labour. Increased productivity and the means of attaining it, *i.e.*, dilution of labour, "scientific management," premium bonus and profit-sharing, workshop committees, etc., are, it will be contended, a capitalist dodge for getting more out of Labour! In many Labour quarters there exists a disposition to lump together for wholesale condemnation, without examination, all proposals which appear to be designed to make industry more productive. Even in pleading for a suspension of this judgment and for more discrimination, I shall here run the risk of being suspected of playing the capitalist game. Nevertheless, it is certain that if any industrial democracy, carrying a substantial improvement in the life of Labour, is to be achieved, great advances in the productivity of Labour are necessary. The assumption that this necessarily involves a painful or injurious intensification of toil on the part of the workers is unwarranted. Increased productivity of industry is not

synonymous with increased toil, though this may seem
to follow from a narrowly conceived idea of Labour as
the source of all wealth.   Improved organisation of
Labour, the invention and application of better
machinery and power, better methods of transport and
marketing, access to better and more abundant
materials, more intelligence and enterprise in the
management, all these and many other factors contribute to enlarged productivity.   But let it be granted
that the full fruits of these other economies are in no
small measure dependent upon the willingness of
workers to remit some of those rules or usages which
in the past have tended to restrict output and to hamper
the best utilisation of the available supplies of labour
for producing wealth.   Is organised Labour going to
use all its strength to secure a complete reversion to
its pre-war attitude, while at the same time seeking
to demand the retention, and a further advance of the
higher standard of wages and of living established
during war-time in most favoured trades.   In other
words, is it going to hamper efforts after increased
productivity, directing its efforts solely to securing for
Labour a larger share of the unenlarged body of wealth,
or will it throw itself into the work of increasing the
national output while at the same time using its
economic and political powers to convert the increased
wealth into higher wages, more freedom, better health,
education, and other opportunities for the nation as
a whole?   Let me briefly state the case for the latter
policy.

The bad and unjust distribution of national wealth
which has hitherto prevailed is not the only vice of
our economic system.   Even had the pre-war income
been equally distributed throughout the nation, there
would not have been enough to secure for the average
family the full requirements of a civilised modern life.
If, after the war, we simply restored the pre-war output,
reckoned at a maximum income of 2,400 million pounds

per annum, we could not, even supposing that all rents, interest, profits, and high salaries were thrown into the common stock, make a fully adequate provision for the popular well-being.   At least 400 millions, or one-sixth of the whole income, would be required to take the shape of savings for the new capital, which under any economic system, Socialist or profiteering, would remain necessary in order to provide for the growing population and requirements of the future.   Further, 400 millions, at least, must go for purposes of national and local government, even assuming that no new social functions were undertaken by the State, no increased military expenditure required, and that the whole burden of war-borrowings was cancelled by taxing the classes who had lent, so as to pay their interest and the sinking fund.   Now 1,600 millions worth of goods and services, the real available net-income, would not, distributed evenly among the population of the United Kingdom, reckoned approximately at 47 millions, yield more than £34 per person, or £136 for an average family of four.   It is, therefore, evident that, even had all the capitalistic pulls upon this income been annulled, the amount of national productivity was not adequate to supply the full requirements of a progressive people.   A civilised Briton wants and can make good use of more than can be bought for £34 a year.

The actual issue of productivity presented to the workers will, however, be far more acute.   A mere return to pre-war productivity would seem to leave the workers worse off than before the war, and definitely worse off than the bulk of them have been during the most prosperous period of the war itself.   For the normal play of economic forces will tell against them in their struggle for a larger proportion of the product. New capital will be relatively scarce and labour relatively abundant.   This means that interest and profit will tend to be high, wages to be low.   The damaged organisation of labour during the war will facilitate this tendency to a fall of real wages, though the fall may be partly concealed by the maintenance of a high level of money wages. If, as is possible, the difficulty of making the pent-up world-demand for goods rapidly effective causes a fall in prices, the attempt to reduce wages from this high war-level will arouse struggles of unprecedented violence, with stoppages of industry that will seriously diminish the national productivity. No temporary victories in such struggles can really serve to win for Labour what it wants—more wealth, more security, more opportunities of life. So far as ordinary private industry is concerned, it is impossible to reduce the market rate of interest and profit in the business world raised by the new conditions of shortage of capital so as to win for labour what it wants—more wealth, more leisure, more security, more opportunities of life. So far as ordinary private industry is concerned, it is impossible to reduce the market rate of interest and profit in the business capital, and to take this sum for the workers in enhanced wages. The attempt to do this is an attempt to apply suddenly in the world of private profiteering enterprise principles of distribution only applicable in a fully Socialist community. Refuse the new capital that is required its high market rate, and one of two things happens. Either it refuses to come into existence (capitalists preferring to spend their income rather than to save it at a low reward), or else it travels abroad and applies itself to work in Argentina, Egypt, India, and China, with labour that is less " exorbitant ' in its demands. Just here, no doubt, will emerge one of the new " nationalist " temptations which the Protectionist-Militarist-Imperialists will dangle before Labour, an embargo or tax upon the export of capital, outside the Empire or the Alliance. This proposal will appear as an adjunct of Protectionism. Just, however, as it will evoke the opposition of powerful financial and commercial interests which have found profit in the development of backward countries, so its superficial appeal to Labour will arouse suspicion when the " national economy " of which it is a part is fully comprehended. The retention of capital within the country, conjoined with tariff protection, will mean the rapid and easy organisation of trusts and other monopolies, the absorption of more capital in labour-saving machinery and the increased " control " of labour by highly organised management, together with a regulation of selling prices which will place once more in the hands of Capital an increased pull on Labour in its capacity of consumer.

Moreover, be it remembered, this " national economy," with its mixture of protection, conservation of capital, guaranteed maximum conditions for labour, is avowedly advocated by politicians and business men as an instrument for that very enhancement of productivity which the worker suspects as a capitalist dodge.

This tangle of cross-issues and appeals can only be safely traversed by Labour taking new soundings and accommodating its policy to the new situation. I claim to have shown that a higher productivity of industry than prevailed before the war is necessary, and that workers will be wise to admit that a considerable increase of output is an indispensable condition of popular progress. What they have to see to is that this increased productivity is accompanied by two conditions. The first is that there must be no net increase of toil or painful effort on the part of Labour, the second that Labour gets as large a share of the increase as circumstances permit. Now by " circumstances ' I do not signify merely the ordinary free play of supply and demand. I include the use of political strength to modify or overrule economic tendencies. This is where the connection between the two problems of the attitude of Labour towards increased productivity on the one hand, and the State upon the other, comes in.

If the State be left out of account, I admit that it will
be very difficult for Labour after the war to have any
security for obtaining the advantages of any increased
productivity it may be asked to promote.   The pre-
sumption, we have seen, is in favour of Capital taking
the lion's share of this after-war product, and, even if
the workers get something out of the enlarged product
in actual wages, they could hardly look forward to any
really considerable improvement of their condition.

It seems, therefore, evident that the workers' share
of increased productivity must depend largely or
mainly upon State policy.   In the first place, the State
will be the employer of labour over vast new fields of
industry.   If, as seems likely, the railways, canals,
and dockyards, a large proportion of the shipping and
shipbuilding trades, the coal and iron mines, the
munition and a large section of the engineering trades,
the liquor trade, together with insurance and banking,
either become fully public industries or remain under
strong State control, as occupations of definitely
" national importance," all questions affecting the
conditions of labour, wages, hours, discipline, demar-
cation, and settlement of disputes, assume a directly
political aspect.   Since these trades comprise a very
large proportion of the best organised employments,
the whole labour situation will be transformed thereby.
The bargaining for improved conditions of employment
will no longer be between trade unions and private
employers, but between trade unions and the State.
Even if some half-way house is found, as in the present
arrangement in the railways and in the other controlled
industries, where the direct management remains in
private hands, the intervention of the State in all
critical decisions may be expected, and both parties
will certainly invoke the political forces open to their
influence.   Even where the industries are left in other
respects to private enterprise, an increasing tendency
for the State to intervene in Labour contracts, and in

matters of hygiene and accident, for the protection of the interests of Labour, has been continually on the increase. Before the war the fixing of minimum piece wages by Trade Boards in an increasing number of "sweated trades" was accompanied by proposals to extend the same method to the great national industry of agriculture.

But these are not the only urgent issues between Labour and the State. The issue of taxation we have recognised as vital. Even were the State called upon to undertake no new expenditure on education and other social services, we see that every year the Government will take something like a tithe of the whole year's product and hand it over to a class of investors, not as payment for the use of current capital, but as blood money. The burden of this new parasitism will add greatly to the total proportion of the product passing to the capitalist class, unless taxation can be so applied that the full incidence of the burden falls upon the capitalist classes themselves. This would probably involve an income tax upon a considerably higher level than that of the war period, because the separate large contribution from war-profits will no longer be available. It is no doubt possible that the railways, the post office, insurance, and other nationalised services may be operated so as to yield a considerable income, independently of taxation, to the State. But it is exceedingly unlikely that such income will accrue to any large extent during the early years of the new experiments. It is more likely that considerable new capital outlays will be needed. The struggle of capitalism to shift the great new burden of war-taxes on to the people by "broadening the basis of taxation," and to stamp upon new proposals of public expenditure for educational and economic developments, will therefore mark a new era in fiscal politics. In this struggle organised Labour must take a hand. For the maintenance of a high standard of public expen-

diture on socially productive services and the issue o
the methods of taxation, by which the ever-growing
public revenue is to be obtained, are of fundamenta
importance to democracy.

CHAPTER IV.

The Conquest of the State.

Summarising the economic situation as it confronts the people, we recognise that new economic functions of the State will be needed to stimulate and support the full employment and the high productivity required to meet the requirements of the situation,

(1) To pay the high interest for capital in private industry and for war debts;

(2) To furnish a high standard of real wages and leisure;

(3) To meet the enlarged requirements of a progressive State in the provision of social services.

This being the situation, the disposition in some Labour quarters to give the go-by to the State, as a capitalist instrument, and to fall back upon new plans of Co-operation, Trade Unionism, Syndicalism, or Guild Socialism, in which the State either plays no part or one of relative unimportance, is seen to be as indefensible as the disposition to reject the movement towards increased productivity. Whatever may be the vices of a capitalist State, there is only one remedy, viz., to convert it into a democratic State. The vision of a working-class organisation building up for itself an economic State, governed by the workers and for the workers, within the political State but virtually independent of that State for the regulation of economic life, is a dangerous phantasy. That Syndicalism and the idea of the self-governing workshop can make a genuine and important contribution to the structural reform of business is everywhere winning admission.

D

Experience of State management and intervention during the war will certainly have strengthened the claim for direct and powerful representation of the workers in the control of businesses more rightly regarded as " belonging to " them than to the owners of the capital invested in them. But, while the old rigidity of State Socialism must be relaxed to allow for the more human interpretation, the idea that the State and its officials can be kept out, or relegated to some unimportant place in the working of industrial democracy, is quite untenable. The economic and the political systems of the nation are destined to be more intimately interdependent than ever. The notion of two States, one a federation of trades and guilds, running the whole body of economic arrangements for the nation by representative committees based upon the common interest of industry, the other a political State, running the services related to internal and external order, and only concerned to intervene in economic affairs at a few reserved points of contact, will not bear criticism. It is commonly bred of political despair, the feeling that the creation of a genuinely democratic State in which the will and interests of the people shall be really paramount is either an impossibility or an ideal too remote for practical consideration.*

But if the common people are to have any power over their material and moral destiny, they must obtain the mastery of the political State and make it into a State whose officials they can trust to do their will and secure their interests. They cannot, in any case, stay the process of State Socialism and the undertaking of an increasing number of important economic functions by the State. If, therefore, they throw their efforts mainly into non-political organisations, they will see

---

* A recent project for Government by Joint Committees of guild representatives and the State (as a consumers' league) is an interesting endeavour to reconcile the inevitable oppositions of economic interests.

these new functions, including such vital services as transport and credit, passing under the power of officials subservient to the profiteering interests that control the present State. Their present well-justified suspicion of the State should be the chief incentive to the task of democratising it. Take a single test. Under present circumstances working men who recognise the folly and the criminality of wars between nations, and are anxious to endow some international government with powers to compel settlement by equitable processes of arbitration, are vehemently opposed to the introduction of any analogous process of compulsory arbitration into industrial disputes. Why? we ask. Why should a group of employees and employers in some single trade, such as mining or railways, disputing about the interpretation of a wage agreement or some other matter affecting their special interests, be allowed to involve in hardship, loss, or ruin the members of other trades and the whole body of consumers, because they insist on fighting out the issue by force instead of submitting it to a public process of justice? The answer is, of course, not that the workers who insist upon the right to strike, really believe that this is the ideal way of settling disputes, but because they distrust the principles, the processes, and the persons who would represent the State in an arbitration. Until a democratic State is won, industrial peace must, therefore, remain impossible, and the general public must submit to the growing perils and damages of an industrial warfare within the nation which will become more bitter and more injurious as the forces of Capital and Labour become better organised, as has happened in military warfare.

Industrial and social safety and progress, therefore, demand the successful capture of the State by the people. This does not only or chiefly mean the predominant power of a Labour or a " populist " party in the House of Commons, with power to compel the Government to adopt democratic measures. A thoroughly democratic franchise is, of course, a first essential to any effective exercise of the people's will. The reform proposals in our electoral system must not merely add more power to the Parliamentary machine, but must greatly improve the quality and the direction of that power. When women are admitted to their full rights and duties as electors and representatives, the great preservative and constructive powers which belong to their sex in the general economy of nature will for the first time make their impress upon the art of politics. The sheer magnitude of this new contribution, changing as it may the very texture of all Government processes, cannot be estimated.

But the stress laid upon the more showy character of elections, Parliamentary representation, and legislative action, must not be allowed to hide from us the important truth that, as the governmental machinery of a great modern State grows in complexity, more and more of the real governing power is of necessity vested in administrative officials. Most modern laws are merely rough sketches, leaving the important concrete substance to be filled in by Orders in Council or departmental fiat. The private personal opinions, sentiments, interests, and attachments of the first-class clerks of the civil services who do this work are, therefore, of determinant importance. Now the drafting, the filling in, and the administration of Acts of Parliament are performed by men who for the most part are born in well-to-do families and have throughout their life consorted exclusively with members of the upper classes. The same is true of the higher and lower grades of the judiciary, before whom come for decision disputed issues of law and fact. The profession to which all the members of the higher Courts belong is, as we have recognised, in its social status and associations the most aristocratic and plutocratic of all, and the anti-popular bias exhibited by highly paid and virtually immovable judges constitutes a grave scandal to the common cause of justice. The small leaven of working-class representatives in the local magistracy goes a very little way towards mitigating the grievance, which is at every stage worsened by the inability of the working-class complainant or defendant to pay the heavy costs of contesting his case on equal terms with his wealthier opponent. This wrong is particularly flagrant in cases relating to disputes between workman and employer, where the lack of power to stand the costs and risks of an appeal to a higher and a more expensive court effectively extinguishes whole grades of justice.

Political democracy, if it is to come into effective being, must grapple successfully with this situation. Men fairly representative of the common interests of the people must be substituted at the focal points for the present guardians of class interests. The civil services, the judiciary and the magistracy as well as the legislature, must be manned by men of the people, if we are to have anything better than the sham self-government which has hitherto prevailed in the so-called Liberal nations of the Western world. Now no sudden popular upheaval of democratic sentiment expressing itself at a general election can achieve this. It stresses a democratic need that is not primarily economic or political—the need of education. As long as the reactionary forces can keep the people from getting a liberal education, they may look with complacency upon every democratic movement. So long as they can keep down the common schooling to the level needed for the clerk or shop assistant, with information and intelligence nicely adapted to the suggestions of their cheap press, they have got " the people " in hand. Half a century ago they were foolishly afraid of a popular franchise and the machinery of democracy. They know better now.

That is why a Speaker's Conference of Liberal and Tory members of Parliament was willing to make large new advances towards a popular representation upon a basis of adult suffrage. Experience has taught them that the working-class movement in politics is innocuous so long as the mind it expresses is the mind of a mob. Their party machinery, their press, their handling of political and social issues, have been continually directed to making and preserving a mob-mind, fluid, sensational, indeterminate, short-sighted, credulous, uncritical. In such a mentality there is no will of the people. Under such conditions it is easy for the ruling and possessing classes to confuse the electorate by dangling before their eyes specious but unsubstantial benefits, to divide them by conflicting appeals to trade or locality, to subject to undetected mutilation any really inconvenient or dangerous reform, and in the last resort to drag across the path of policy some great inflammatory national appeal to passion. Until the people evolve an intelligent will capable of resisting these influences, a real democracy continues to be impossible.

Better and purer education is the first essential. This does not imply a high standard of intellectual culture generally diffused throughout the people. We need not deceive ourselves by false assumptions of equality in human nature. It may well be the case that the majority in every grade of society is not susceptible to the appeals of a definitely intellectual life. What is needed is such free access to intellectual opportunities as shall produce in every social environment a considerable minority of able and informed minds, and a majority whose minds are sufficiently intelligent to choose, to trust, and to follow the leadership of this intellectual minority. Common sense for the many, a wide intellectual outlook for the few, and a popular will to which both contribute—these are the requirements. Though the organised instruc-

tion of schools and colleges only forms a part of the
needed education (mainly comprised of personal experience in the home, the workshop, and the neighbour-
hood) it is an exceedingly important part for the purpose
which we are immediately considering., viz., political
power.   For a new series of conflicts are going to be
fought round the Education Question.   We have
already seen that the ruling and possessing classes
recognise the necessity of some sort of higher education
for those whom in playful derision they have called
" their masters."   The modern technique of popular
capitalism demands not only a larger measure of
specialised manual skill, but some slight scientific
knowledge and some trained capacity of thinking for
large numbers of employees.   Employers have learned
that high technical efficiency requires some cultivation
of general intelligence.   Their problem, as we saw, is
to prevent this education of general intelligence from
becoming a source of dangerous class-consciousness.
This can be done, their educationalists think, by intro-
ducing certain " wholesome " influences into the
processes of education and producing a certain atmosphere.   This issue is no novel one.   The hold of the
churches on the schools has always had as one of its
aims the use of spiritual soporifics to allay the discontent
of the poor with their humble status.   This has been
the special service always rendered by the Church to
the ruling classes in the State.   But the reactionists,
recognising that religion has lost a good deal of its
ancient hold upon the masses, plan a more audacious
policy.   They propose to impose their own social
dogmas — Militarism, Imperialism, Protectionism,
exclusive Nationalism—as a new religion upon the
teaching and discipline of the schools of the people.
Everywhere in the teaching of history, geography, or
literature the emotional bias of " patriotism " is to
prevail, while the elements of civics, and even of
biology, are to be exploited so as to impress class

discipline, national pride, the duties of prolific
parentage, race hostility, and to divide popular
solidarity at every stage by presenting life as a
competitive struggle instead of a human co-operation.
Not only is this "religion" to pervade our teaching,
but it is to be enforced by military and patriotic rites
and exercises upon the plastic mind of the young
citizen. This prussic acid is already being pumped into
our boys and girls, with the object of quenching the
spirit of liberty in thought and action. The human
mind is not to be trained to the free handling of facts
and their disinterested interpretation, but to be cribbed,
cabined, and confined by the acceptance of a selected,
distorted, and impassioned view of the world in which
we live and our conduct in it. Military drill, the
worship of the flag, Empire day, and other "national"
Saints' days, the whole tenor of the *esprit de corps*
and the "atmosphere" of school life are to be directed
to produce effective fighting patriotism. If reactionists are allowed to hold these intellectual and moral
fortresses, they can afford to snap their fingers at the
working-class movement in industry and politics. For
the people will not be able to produce the minority of
liberal-minded leaders they require, and the common
sense needed for the compact majority of followers will
have been poisoned at the source.

Nor is it only a question of the elementary schools.
The whole system of secondary education and the new
universities to which the people have access in our
great industrial centres will, if permitted, be turned
into forcing houses for Militarism, Imperialism, and
exclusive Nationalism, and the teaching of history,
economics, and civics will be insidiously directed to
construct intellectual defences against the inroads of
democracy. If democracy is to have any chance of
survival and growth, the fight for liberty and purity of
education must be fought and won without delay. For
the war will leave an aftermath of popular suspicion,

credulity, and animosity particularly favourable to the intellectual and moral cause of reaction. The herd-mind which years of national peril and of conflict has evoked may easily be induced to commit itself to after-war policies fatal to personal liberty, to peace, and to democracy. To maintain the fears and fervours of this herd-mind, and to turn them into grist for the capitalist-bureaucratic-military mill is the avowed intention of the spokesmen of reaction. School, press, church, party, will all be dragged into the service, and the money of plutocratic donors will furnish the supplementary funds and evoke the desired intellectual response.

I am not here writing a general treatise upon education, but discussing it in its special bearing upon the struggle for democracy in the immediate future. We approached the subject from a recognition of the need for the democratisation of the administrative services, recognising that so long as these posts were left as a preserve of the well-to-do classes, popular government was not attainable. Equality of educational opportunities is one key to this position. But another is reform of educational methods and values. Here are two dangers, two diverse and opposing plans by which reactionism has striven to defend itself. One is the retention of obsolete mediæval curricula, the artificial culture of a leisured master class, exhibiting its unearned wealth in ostentatiously useless and decorative "accomplishments." If a small minority of clever working-class boys can by judicious selection be brought into this atmosphere of higher education, such an opening of opportunity will be far from harmful to the oligarchy. It will draw from the service of the people the picked brains of their sons and fit them for the work of helping to manage the people. This has been the method hitherto found satisfactory. Certain concessions to modernism have been made in subjects and methods of teaching, but the social and intellectual atmosphere of higher education in all its stages has been kept immune from dangerous influences. The new pressure for popular opportunities can, however, be rendered innocuous in another way. Instead of directing the latent intellectualism of the workers into enervating paths of class-culture, it is possible to press it into utilitarian moulds, by over-stressing the importance of the applied sciences and purely technical accomplishments to the detriment of any broad personal culture. This seems to be a doubly advantageous defence of capitalism. For while, on the one hand, it directs the people's intelligence from the sorts of knowledge that yield political power, on the other, it harnesses their brains, as well as their muscles, to the chariot of profiteering industry.

Democracy must, therefore, prepare for two great struggles in the field of education; one against the attempt to keep down to a low level the national expenditure on humane and civic culture, while making due provision for scientific and technical instruction of a directly utilitarian order; the other against the degradation of such human and civic culture as is provided, by the intrusions of sedatives and stimuli devised for interested purposes of " defence."

CHAPTER V.

The Close State *versus* Internationalism.

This great struggle between the forces of democracy and those of the capitalist oligarchy will not be permitted to appear so definite in its outlines as it is here presented. For, if the people could really get to feel and understand how much is at stake, such feeling and understanding would vastly strengthen that subtle and imponderable element, the conscious will to victory. An accurate instinct of class self-defence will, therefore, lead the reactionists to do all that is possible to obscure the issue, and in particular to pretend (or even to believe) that they are not fighting against democracy or for the defence of class power and privilege. Their most conscious tactics have been long foreshadowed under the loose title of Tory Democracy. These tactics will be directed to two main ends. The first is to confine the political and economic movements of Labour within the limits of nationality, expelling the elements of internationalism. The second is to conserve their own political and economic supremacy within the nation by every sort of concession—economic, social, and political—consistent with the maintenance of that supremacy. Such is the "national" policy at the head of which, in this country, Mr. Lloyd George (or his successor) will place himself. It will offer a whole world of socialistic and democratic reforms, on condition that the people fall down and worship it. I have already indicated its nature under the description of Prussian-Australianism. It will be replete with boons and benefits to the working classes, guaranteed standard wages, limited hours of labour, provision against unemployment, better housing, free medical service, access to the land, facilities for co-operative enterprise in agriculture and industry, and "a voice" in the control of the workshops and the trade on matters affecting Labour, combined with "scientific management" under various designations.   There will be adult suffrage for men and women, minority representation, possibly a referendum.   A castrated Labour Government may even seem to be a possibility of the near future.

Only one general condition will be appended—that of close nationalism, the organised national or imperial State, self-sufficing in all the essentials of government, economics, and defence.   Internationalism in the shape of Mr. Wilson's and Lord Grey's League of Nations is not, we shall be told, a presently practicable idea : the stern facts of life in a dangerous world forbid a nation or an empire like our own to place its destiny outside the limits of its own control. Such international alliances as it may cultivate must, therefore, be confined to chosen friends and must in no case involve anything in the nature of international government.   Our empire must be the largest area of organisation : to the development of its resources and the cultivation of its sentiment of unity all considerations of foreign relations must be subordinated.   This nation and this empire must be strengthened by special measures of a constructive and corporate kind. There must be concerted action for imperial defence, involving the maintenance of conscription and of a great standardised military and naval power.   The necessity of this defence, derived from the refusal of internationalism, will itself involve the formation of a close imperial federal State, in which the world-politics, hitherto controlled by a British Foreign Office, will be delegated to a representative imperial Cabinet or Council, in which the self-governing dominions will be called in to guarantee the orderly subjection and the profitable exploitation of the subject peoples in India, our Crown Colonies, and our Protectorates.* Protectionism, primarily, as we saw, a special brand of capitalist plundering, will be presented as a necessary measure of defence, as a policy of imperial and national organisation. We must have all our " key " industries under our own flag. Public finance, as well as commerce, must be developed (upon German lines) for this scientific exploration and exploitation of the empire. The necessity of having ample supplies of all important foods and materials within our political area of control will impel us to new measures of imperial expansion in competition with rival empires, for rich supplies of copper, iron, rubber, oil, cotton, nitrates, discovered in unappropriated backward countries.

Now it is idle to deny that such a scheme has powerful appeals to the more innocent and uninstructed workers in this country, as in France and Germany. In all countries some Labour leaders can be won over to adopt it as the largest, safest, and most immediate measure of Socialism and democracy that is available, and a large support will be given by a rank and file whose mind is still inflamed by the passions of the war. The atmosphere of envy, hatred, malice, and suspicion will be favourable for fastening a separatist system upon our politics and trade, and for " keeping ourselves to ourselves " by setting up barriers against " the foreigner," visualised primarily by the Hun, but easily extended to include all nations who did not fight upon our side in the great war. Hitherto, we shall be told, the nations of the Western world, and Britain especially, have been drifting rapidly towards an economic internationalism, the peril of which has been exposed by the war. Safety, progress, and social

* The Empire Resources Development Committee, upon which sit five members of our Government, has an interesting scheme for " imperialising " the land of our tropical dependencies and forcing natives to grind dividends for companies and revenue for the State.

demócracy can only be realised within the limits of the national or imperial State, for only within these limits can the political organisation which Socialism requires be made available. A nation, to be strong and safe, must rely upon its own economic and human resources. The working-class " international " is little more than a vague humanitarian sentiment. It is and will remain devoid of political or economic reality. Of the two opposing forces, Capitalism and Socialism, it is the former, not the latter, which is in its proclivities international. French logic poses the issue in the following sharp antithesis:

> " Capitalism needs peace in order to live and grow: it is international in essence and in organisation. Socialism, upon the other hand, though it may hate war, has nothing that is inconsistent with the narrowest nationalism. It is a pure accident that it has hitherto affected, especially in France, a humanitarian and internationalist form. It is national Socialism that must rank as the least chimerical and the most logical of Socialisms. For Socialism can only be realised theoretically in a closed State, shut within stiff barriers, whose economic equilibrium is not liable constantly to be upset by external occurrences."*

The practical failure of the international factor of Socialism in August, 1914, will be taken as testimony to its merely sentimental character. Working-class Socialists who mean business must therefore build upon the broadest practical foundation open to them—their national organisation. They will be told, " You have your national resources under your own control, if you organise your political and economic power. The war has achieved a large measure of State Sociálism, which you have only to retain and to administer for working-

---

* Alfred de Tarde, " L'Europe Court-Elle à sa Ruine? " p. 25.

class purposes. The British self-governing Dominions have already committed themselves to this path of advance. March with them in working out an imperial social democracy, without waiting for the more backward nations to achieve the slow and difficult task of achieving a level of political liberty which will make the international union a possibility.''

Such a plea for close nationalism, however, will only seem plausible so long as it remains in the region of general phrases. Can the civilisation of the world henceforth live in separate national compartments? Though political internationalism has not gone very far, economic internationalism has. The whole material and moral fabric of modern life is laid in a most elaborate network of commercial, physical, and personal communications by which the members of all advanced States have been brought into close and continual co-operation for many of the essential services and activities. To withdraw from these communications, or in any way to weaken them, would be a signal damage to the life even of the French people, who are more self-sufficient for the essential services of life—economical and moral—than any other great European nation. For Great Britain the shock and injury of such a reversal of her activities would be incalculably great. The entire body of our economic system, on its productive and consumptive sides, has been nourished upon the freest available access to all markets, all national supplies, all economic opportunities throughout the world. A large and growing proportion of our wealth has been obtained by organising and controlling the supply of international communications—transport, commercial, and financial. We cannot achieve the close imperialism or nationalism to which we are invited without abandoning these great and profitable functions of internationalism. The closer economic unity of the Empire could furnish no compensation for such a surrender of our wider economic *rôle*. That Empire

cannot be converted into a " close " economic system
capable of furnishing all the requirements of its inhabi-
tants from its own areas, vast and varied though they
are.   A single test-fact will suffice to prick any such
pretence.   Four-fifths of our wheat supply comes from
overseas.   Now in a year of bad harvest, 1908, our
Empire only furnished 24 per cent. (less than one-
quarter) of our importation of this necessity of life.
Almost the whole supply of some of the necessary
materials for our staple manufactures, such as cotton,
rubber, petroleum, nitrates, and potash are drawn, and
must for a long time be drawn, from countries outside
our Empire.   Any experiment in a close imperial or
national   system,   supported   by   Protection,   must
grievously impair our access to these foreign sources
of supply which have hitherto poured into our open
ports.   Though Free Trade has historically been
associated with a capitalist economy, no British State,
however Socialistic in its inner structure, could afford
to tamper with the free importation of foreign goods
or to confine within artificial barriers the operation of
British shipping and finance.

The first objection, therefore, to close nationalism or
imperialism is that it is unsafe and impracticable from
the economic standpoint.   Another objection, equally
vital, is that such a " Socialism " as it promises could
not be democratic.   It is, in fact, part of a design to
substitute a new sort of Capitalism under the name of
State Socialism, for the competing Capitalism which
had reached its zenith and was doomed to pass away.
Under this State Socialism the ruling and possessing
classes would retain their power, their property, and
their profitable control of the workers.   Great land-
lords like Lord Derby, mining and rail magnates like
Lord Rhondda, prosperous capitalists in grocery or
newspapers, like Lord Devonport and Lord North-
cliffe, would continue in peace, as in war, to organise
the national resources in the name of a State which

had thrown off all real control of Parliament and the electorate, and consisted of a confederacy of these big business men with their permanent staffs of civil servants and their changing staffs of politicians to do the necessary legislative business in conformity with the empty usages of representative government. This new capitalism would be stronger and more profitable than the old. For the trades it ruled would take two shapes. Some would be State monopolies, in which high wages of management would form the smallest part of the spoils, the great " profiteering " opportunities being found in the subsidiary trades contracting for the State monopolies. The real strongholds of profiteering would be found in the cartels and syndicates which, in close imitation of Germany, would soon emerge as the results of a union of State control and Protectionism, and in the restoration of a British Junker Squiredom flourishing upon the high rents of a subsidised and protected agriculture. The aim would be to secure such State control as is consistent with the largest liberty and opportunity of private profiteering. If wasteful competition within each primary industry can be repressed and Labour can be coerced, cajoled, or bribed into a policy of better discipline and higher productivity, a solid foundation for this new capitalism is laid. It will be said that this presumes overmuch upon the submissiveness of Labour and its blindness to the meaning of the new bondage. But here comes in the contribution of other reactionary forces. The experiment in war policy is itself a rough draft of what the new capitalism requires. The problem is how to extend and consolidate this system as a permanent peace policy. In order to succeed in this it would seem necessary to retain, as far as possible, the motives and stimuli so effectively applied for the duration of the war. This means the retention of the general feeling that we are living in a dangerous world and that we are liable at any time to be sub-

jected to the perils of another war. If this war were
really made " the war to end war," and were followed
by an era of security, general disarmament, and the
development of a solid international order, the new
capitalist world would be unattainable. The attempt
is, therefore, certain to be made (not with clear, conscious intention, but by the drift of selfish interests
which we have seen to be the ordinary *modus operandi*)
to keep this country and the Western world in a
sufficiently unsettled state to reconcile the workers to
the necessary subjugations and restraints. This is the
chief significance of the Paris Economic Conference,
its economic supports for the present alliance after
peace is concluded, its boycott of the Central Powers
and all the accompanying Protectionism. The effort,
and the implicit purpose, is to stop the resumption of
free international commerce, to set up lasting economic
conflicts in Europe, and so to render impossible a
League of Nations. This policy would ensure a
dangerous world. It would justify the maintenance of
military conscription and great competing armaments,
thus providing for the discipline of the working classes
and the forcible repression of any proletarian movement, economic or political, which threatened the
public order. While playing directly into the hands of
the great armament businesses, it would also furnish
the requisite stimuli and instruments for the further
pursuit of an imperial aggrandisement which in its
turn would evoke the competition of other aspiring
empires and so once more react against security and
internationalism.

While, therefore, a closed State, national or
imperial, might be Socialistic in economic structure,
it could not be democratic in government. For it is
not only actual war that is seen to be incompatible
with democracy. Potential war is seen to be likewise
incompatible. Now the Nationalism, Imperialism,
Militarism, Protectionism of a " closed State " are

potential war. They are a reversion to a state of things which, regarded from the international and human standpoint, is literally anarchy. Such industrial harmony, or Socialism, as might conceivably exist inside this closed State must be subordinated to considerations of national defence. Its primary function must be to contribute the maximum economic strength for the emergency of war. Its industry, transport, commerce, and finance would be organised with this end consciously in view. Only such " social reforms " as contribute to this end could be adopted. Rural development would aim exclusively at food supplies for a besieged country and a large, sturdy population for cannon-food. Railways and roads would be primarily strategic. Mining, engineering, shipbuilding, chemical, and other industries of direct military or naval value would be controlled, subsidised, and otherwise artificially stimulated, such favourable terms of employment being accorded as would maintain an adequate supply of highly productive labour. Other occupations would be graded as of greater or less national importance, according to their presumptive utility, material or financial, for purposes of war. Commerce would, so far as feasible, be confined for all essentials to the limits of the nation or the empire, for non-essentials to a restricted circle of allied or friendly Powers. Shipping would be directed by State-owned, controlled, or subsidised lines along imperial and other prescribed routes. The intellectual and spiritual life of the closed State would be regulated by an educational policy, a press and art censorship, a religious and a recreational system, prescribed by political power and enforced by all the modes of authority and influence which we have already explored. Not only the material life of the people, but its soul, would thus be nationalised and militarised under the closed State. Democracy could have no place in such a State. In industry, as in politics, the Government, dominated in all matters of importance by considerations not of general human welfare but of national defence qualified by business pulls, must impose the arbitrary will of political and business rulers and their paid experts upon the people. Though the forms of popular self-government might survive, and even be extended, not merely in the field of politics, but of industry, the dominant purpose of the closed State would quench the spirit of popular control wherever it asserted itself. For the closed State must remain a military State, and all the sacrifices which the people have made in war would be riveted upon them in the intervals of rest from war, entitled peace.

This diagnosis will seem to some an exaggeration. Possibly it is. For it presents the logic of the closed State, working more clearly and cleanly than would be the case in Great Britain. The evolution of this new national order would emerge blurred and crossed by conflicting tendencies. The capitalistic forces, as we know, would be themselves divided. Those with international associations would struggle against the rigid nationalisation of the new order, and might make common cause with the more enlightened sections of Labour. This division of capitalist forces has served in recent years to retard the evolution of the reactionary movement in this country, not only towards protec·tionism, but towards militarism, bureaucracy, and the close State. After the war strong elements of this opposition may still survive, and by means of *ad hoc* co-operation with the Socialist workers may put heavy obstacles in the path of the constructive policy of reaction. In thus acting, their particular trade interests will be fortified by a recognition that the costs of the expensive militarist-protectionist policy must chiefly fall on them. Trades which possess a profitable pull upon the State, in tariffs, subsidies, and public con·tracts, may meet the high income and property taxes that must be imposed with a smiling face, for they get more than they give. But the capitalists whose trades either are dependent largely upon free · international trade and finance, or else are so distinctively domestic that Protection is of no use to them, will have to meet the high taxation with no compensating advantages. When they come to realise this situation and to understand that by no fiscal devices can they shift on to the workers the bulk of the new tax-burden, many of those capitalists will be likely to come over to a pacifist internationalist frame of mind. This probable division in the business world may prove of critical importance in weakening the solidarity of capitalism.

But it remains none the less true that the survival of democracy must depend in the long run upon a new, determined, and intelligent rally of the forces of Labour to the cause of Internationalism. For the full effort of the Unholy Alliance will be directed to enlist the sympathy and interests of Labour for this project of a close State. The emotional atmosphere will be favourable. National and imperial self-reliance will make a popular appeal. The public guarantees of high money-wages and other good conditions will be represented as contingent upon a " national economy " which shall exclude cheap foreign labour and its produce from our shores. The inevitable costs of this " economy," viz., reduced income, precarious supplies of foreign foods and materials, expensive armaments, recurring war-peril, conscription, capitalist bureaucracy, will be concealed as far as possible. Carefully selected drafts of labour men will from time to time be taken over into the bureaucracy, a process which will be presented as an adequate response to the demand for a democratic organisation of industry. In fact it will be designed to serve, and will serve, as an inoculation against what officialism regards as the disease of democracy.

The peril of this endeavour to debauch the working-class movement cannot be met by a mere exposure of the capitalistic-bureaucratic-militarist policy. The mere recognition of the fact that the ruling and possessing castes are playing their old game of substituting a vertical national cleavage for a lateral class cleavage will not furnish an adequate resistance. The so-called international solidarity of Labour is too distinctively sentimental a force, and the idea of an international class war conducted on the industrial field by a general strike or any other mode of simultaneous revolt against capitalism, is almost as remote from practicability as the kindred proposal to stop a war by a simultaneous refusal of the workers to respond to the call to arms. I do not under-value the importance of getting the workers, who are also the peoples of the different countries, to confer, to unite, and to take concerted action when they can. But the identity of interest between the working classes of the different nations in " the class struggle " does not in itself yet afford the requisite community of thought and feeling for powerful international co-operation. It is not supported by a sufficient body of close personal intercourse and the sort of understanding which can come in no other way. It is very difficult for workers whose languages and ways of living are so different and whose opportunties of meeting one another are so narrowly confined, to fuse directly in any powerful international movement upon a mere basis of community of occupation. Education and growing intercourse between the active working-class leaders of the respective nations may in time do much. But at present it is too precarious a bond for the internationalism which is so urgently required. For the immediate enemy, as we see, will be the close State. And working-class internationalism has continually oscillated between the policy of ignoring the State, while trying to build up an economic internationalism outside it, and the policy of using the State for definitely economic ends. Even Socialism, though international in theory, has seldom set itself to any conception of the necessity of an international movement of political democracy, a concerted movement towards a mastery of the national State by the workers of the respective nations, with the object of building up an international democracy. Yet this is precisely the work that must be done, if democracy is to survive. Any endeavour to build up industrial democracy either on a national or an international basis merely or mainly by means of working-class organisation outside State machinery must fail. Industrial and political democracy stand or fall together, by an insepar-able fate. If the workers within each nation cannot capture their State, and through their State the new international political arrangements, League of Nations, or whatever it be called, they will be helpless in the hands of their rulers and their capitalists. Trade Unionism, Syndicalism, or Guild Socialism, therefore, though containing contributions of inestimable value towards democracy, cannot provide a short cut or dispense with the necessity of seizing, reforming, and democratising the machinery of existing States and inter-State relations.

For all the actual transactions which imperil peace and so sustain militarism and bureaucracy within each country will continue to be governmental, and unless the peoples can control their Governments, that control will continue to be exercised by the combination of business and political forces permanently hostile to peace and internationalism.

The temptation to shun the State instead of mastering it has come up recently in a particularly dangerous shape—that of a refusal to support the new proposal for founding inter-State relations upon a League of Nations, because the Governments which would form and operate this League would not at first be democratic in their constitution. How is it possible,

we are told, that you can entrust safely the beginnings
of such an international Government to the very class
of men in the several countries whose aggressive and
suspicious temper, class interests, obsolete and incom-
petent statecraft, have got the world into its present
desperate plight?   The answer is that, though no high
measure of security may be attained under such conditions, the insecurity of the only present alternative,
viz., a reversion to the pre-war situation of two opposing
groups under the control of these same men, is far
more formidable.   We cannot suppose that the business
of the world can be conducted without any formal and
collective   arrangements   between   the   constituent
nations.   Many of those arrangements must be conducted by the Governments of those nations.   It is
surely safer that the Governments which will conduct
these arrangements shall be on formally amicable terms
than arrayed in hostile groups or alliances.   Just as
the vices and defects of a class government within a
nation rightly constitute a challenge and an incentive
to popular control, so likewise with the international
Government.   An ill-constructed State is generally
better than anarchy.   Now the only present alternative
to a League of Nations, however unsatisfactory in its
personal control, is a return to international anarchy.
Democratic control of the Society of Nations, as of the
several nations, is the only full security for peace and
progress, but that is no ground for refusal to support
the best beginnings of that international society which,
under the existing circumstances, are attainable.   It
is not true that the formation of a League of Nations,
binding themselves to enforce by common action the
fulfilment of their treaty obligations, places a new
weapon in the hands of the ruling classes and constitutes a new danger to the workers.   If such a League,
however undemocratically controlled, is effective in its
main object, it reduces the aggregate of military and
naval force in the world and lessens the likelihood of

its use. The danger of a class Government within a nation using its armed forces to repress strikes or other popular movements will be diminished proportionately with the reduction of national armaments, which will be the result and measure of the success of the League. The notion of the League turning into a new Holy Alliance of the capitalist bureaucracy within each State for the concerted repression of all democratic movements can hardly be a serious apprehension in face of the divergencies of interest between the ruling groups within the several States. But even if such a danger were latent in the formation of an international Government, it would be better for democracy to confront it than to lapse into the pre-war situation definitely worsened by the new powers wielded by reaction within each State.

The sound policy for each people is to accept and welcome the formation of a League of Nations, however imperfect in representation, as an instrument for the operation of the larger international will so soon as that will becomes real enough to master the instrument. There is, however, no reason why the more advanced nations should acquiesce even at the outset in an undemocratic constitution of a League of Nations. It is certainly of grave importance that the traditions of the bad statecraft of the past should be scrapped and that the effective relations between States in the future should be conducted by men and methods reflecting the national interests and common welfare of the peoples involved. This can only be compassed by provisions in the constitution of the Courts, Councils, or other international bodies formed to secure the peace and promote the common good of nations, for the appointment of persons genuinely representative, in knowledge, capacity, and interests, of the popular life of the several countries. Whether such appointments should be made directly by popular representation among the several peoples, or by election of their Parliaments, is not of vital importance. For unless the people is vigorous and intelligent enough to secure the mastery of their own national State, they cannot hope to control their international representatives upon the League of Nations, and the importance of the latter achievement ought to be an additional incentive to the former. It is the same current of democratic energy that has to flow into and nourish the organs of national and international government. To refuse the second of these related tasks, or to attempt to substitute for it some distinctively non-political form of internationalism, would be a fatal error that would play into the hands of the reactionists by enabling the enemies of democracy to establish the close militarist protected State and to cajole or coerce the people into defending it as the only tolerable method of security. in a world which they will purposely keep dangerous in order that their class policy may continually impose itself on popular credulity.

.   .   .   .

Such is the issue as I see it emerging from the fog of war. The forces of reaction will be more closely consolidated than before, more conscious of their community of interest and of the part which they respectively can play in the maintenance of "social order." They will have had recent and striking testimony to the submissive and uncritical character of the people, and of their own ability to impose their arbitrary will upon the conduct of affairs in which the popular temper was supposed to be most sensitive. They will have at their disposal a large number of new legal instruments of coercion and the habits of obeying them derived from several years of use. The popular mind will have been saturated with sentiments and ideas favourable to a constructive policy of national defence, Imperialism, Protectionism, and bureaucratic Socialism making for a close State under class control with the empty forms of representative government. All the educative and suggestive institutions—church, schools and universities, press, places of amusement—will be poisoned with false patriotism, and class domination masquerading as national unity.

On the other hand, a powerful fund of genuine democratic feeling will be liberated with the peace. The temper of the peoples, released from the tension of war, will be irritable and suspicious, and this irritability and suspicion, copiously fed by stories of Governmental incompetence and capitalistic greed in the conduct of the war, and sharpened by personal sacrifices and privations, will be dangerous for Governments. The contrast between the liberties for which they were fighting and the new restraints to which they are subjected will be disconcerting and instructive. Every trade and every locality will have its special difficulties and grievances. Economic and financial troubles will everywhere break up the artificial national unity of war-time, and the grave political cleavages that must display themselves when the issues of taxation, permanent conscription, State ownership of industries, imperial federation, and international relations open out, will, by breaking the old moulds of party, set free large volumes of political energy for new experiments in political and economic reconstruction, Many of the old taboos of class prestige, sex distinction, sanctity of property, and settled modes of living and thinking, will be broken for large sections of the population. The returning armies will carry back into their homes and industries powerful reactions against militarism, and will not be disposed to take lying down the attempt of the reactionists to incorporate it as a fixed institution in the State. In every country of Europe popular discontent will be seething and suspicions against rulers gathering. In other words, all the factors of violent or pacific revolution will exist in conscious activity. The raw material and energy for a great democratic movement will be at hand, provided that thought, organisation, and direction can make them effective. Hitherto for our working, as indeed for our other classes, clear thinking has been an intolerable burden. But there is no congenital racial incapacity for thinking, if the emergency is adequate, and, for the workers, at any rate, it should be adequate. For they will be confronted by the now plain alternative of a firmly entrenched class-supremacy in politics, industry, and every other social institution, and the necessity of popular organisation for the control of the Government in order that they may recover their lost liberties and establish and extend the principles of political and social self-government.

www.ingramcontent.com/pod-product-compliance
Lightning Source LLC
Chambersburg PA
CBHW021534270326
41930CB00008B/1251